Greatness
is a Process

27 Suggestions to Bring Out the Greatness Within You

RUFFUS J. YATES, IV

Copyright © 2017 Ruffus J. Yates, IV

Published by Shari Quinn Publishing

To order additional copies of this title, contact your favorite bookstore

Edited by Shari W. Quinn

Cover Illustrated by Ruffus J. Yates

Interior Design by Shari W. Quinn

ISBN-13: 978-1978250307
ISBN-10: 1978250304

Greatness Is A Process

TABLE OF CONTENTS

Dedication i

Introduction 1

Focus On What is Important 2

Never Mind The Sidelines 4

Build In Silence..6

Health Is Wealth..8

Less Is More...10

Procrastination 12

Assumptions...14

To Observe Will not Hurt 16

Work Smart 18

Break Bad Habits...20

Sacrifice 22

Discipline 24

Educate Yourself..25

Have Faith..27

Chase Your Dreams...29

Productive Hobbies..30

Weigh Your Options..31

Know Your Worth 32

Embrace The Struggle 34

Speak Highly Of Yourself 36

Travel...37

Set Goals 39

Do not Expect Handouts...40

Never Look Back 41

Stay Positive...42

Think Before You Make A Move 44

Do What Makes You Happy 46

About The Author 49

Dedication

A special thank you to my parents, Rufus Yates and Shari Quinn; grandparents, family and friends; to the South End neighborhood where I was raised, and the city of Albany, New York, where I was born.

Introduction

"They hate you when you are winning, but they love you. When you break ... this is the price of being great. - Meek Mill"

I wrote this book as a self-help resource book for myself and others that want the best for themselves. This is a reminder to never give up and work incredibly hard for what you want. You can do anything you put your mind to, therefore you should never settle for less. It is important to do what makes you happy and make yourself proud. It is never too late to change for the better. Everything in this book comes from life lessons that I learned first-hand. I turned the negatives into a positive, and learned significant insight from observing and listening. I hope this book allows you to do the same.

Focus On What is Important

"I do not focus on what I'm up against. I focus on my goals and I try to ignore the rest." - Venus Williams

Time is the most expensive item in the world, spend it wisely. It is easy to get distracted by what is going on around you. You will find yourself lost trying to keep up with what is going on. In order to focus thoroughly on something, you must first know what it is that you want to focus on. You must prioritize. If something is not helping you, then it is taking away from you. Eliminate all distractions, whether it is social media or social events. Focus on your goals, and once you accomplish them, all of the things you wanted to indulge in will still be there. Do what you need to do now so you can do what you want later in life. You must have the determination to stay the course until the task is complete.

The number one reason people fail is from their inability to remain focused. Get up every morning and grind. For each minute you are worried about the opinions of others, it is time that you have lost. Refuse to be moved by

things that do not help you achieve your goals. Each level you climb, the distractions will increase. Master your mind. Keep your eyes on the prize. Life is a marathon, not a race. Be single-mindedly focused.

What are you going to do today to improve your life? A disciplined mind can do the impossible. How well you master the art of staying focused will determine how great you will be. Every time you are distracted it takes away your precious time and even more time to regain focus, regardless whether it is four minutes, four hours or four weeks.

Never Mind The Sidelines

"Whomever is trying to bring you down
is already beneath you." - Unknown

It does not matter what you do or how you choose to live your life. Whether you are doing good or bad, there will always be someone to judge you or find a flaw to securitize and try to capitalize from it. You have to look ahead and know that life is like a race. If you turn to the sidelines to address someone who is trying to ridicule you, others will far surpass you in the race. There is no time to negotiate, converse nor entertain a hater. They are objective is to trick you out of your premier spot merely because they want to be in your place. If you cannot handle being negatively talked about, then you cannot handle being great. Disregard what other people think of you. There is no point in stressing over something you have no control over. Time is still ticking.

Do not waste your day on people who cannot enhance your future. Leave them where they belong. Try to limit the amount of time you spend with people who judge, gossip, speculate or ridicule. Choose to primarily surround yourself with positive, inspiring influencers. You cannot bring every one with you, everyone has a purpose in your life.

Some have a purpose is to distract you from obtaining a certain of level of greatness that is already within you. Un-comfortability makes you grow. Learn how to stay calm. Never mind what haters say, ignore them until they disappear. When you feed into it, you are only adding fuel to their fire. Bury your enemies with greatness. Stop letting people who do so little for you control so much of your mind, energy and emotion.

Build In Silence

"When you build in silence, people
do not know what to attack." -
Anonymous

When you are working on yourself you
must do it in silence and let your results
speak for itself. Forty-nine per cent of
people will pray for your downfall. Likewise,
49 per cent will try and talk you out if it
because they do not think they can do it
themselves, and they certainly do not want to
see you achieve it. People will attempt to
project their fears on you. Once you have
made your mind up that you want to do
something, do it silently. The less people
who know your dreams and plans, the better.
Try not to be so eager to tell people your
every move. Believe in yourself even when
no one else does.

Surprisingly, sometimes you even have to
keep good news to yourself. You must be

your own biggest fan. Eventually people will see the

what you been working so hard on. They do not need to see the painstaking practice or the sleepless nights you endured to get where you are or where you are headed.

Make your accomplishments seem effortless. Relentlessly work hard while They are asleep. Work while They are partying. When you tell someone what you are going to do, you are only giving them a chance to prepare for it. Catch people by surprise. Keep everything in your head until all the work is done, and sit back and watch everyone wonder how you did it. Not everything you want to say needs to be said.

Health Is Wealth

"It is health that is the real wealth." –
Gandhi

When you look good, you feel good. Take care of your body, physically, mentally and emotionally. Preserve your energy, and do not waste it on the wrong things. People can be toxic and drain all your energy, if you let them. Health is much more imperative than wealth. A rich person can purchase nice cars, houses, and other materialistic items but one can only enjoy these luxuries if they are in good health and a good state of mind. You do not have to vigorously exercise. Fresh air helps us improve our immune system and overall health. Try your hardest to stay stress-free as stress weakens your immune system and increases your chances of health issues. Do not stress over things you cannot change. If you have spare time go sign up for a gym membership,

invest ten dollars a month to go to the gym, it is certainly worth it. You should want to glow, not only mentally and financially but physically as well.

Less Is More

"Sometimes your circle decreases in size but increases in value" - Unknown

There is power in quality, not quantity. It does not matter how many friends you have. However, it does matter how many of those friends you can depend on in your time of need. My grandmother always used to say, "A friend in need, is a friend indeed."

Further, the more friends you have, the more people you have distracting you from what is important. You should look at a person's value and their effect on your well-being and your life. Friends effect your happiness and health, good or bad.

Friends will either lift you or bring you down. Choose wisely; remember who supported you and who switched up. When you go through adversity, people will show you

their true colors. When people show you their true colors, do not be color-blind nor try to paint a different picture. A leopard does not change their spots, if someone does something once, it is a high probability that they will do it again.

Lions hunt alone! Be careful of the company you keep. Do not hang around other people just because you are insecure with yourself. Find your inner confidence, everyone has it, you just have to pull it out. No one was born with super powers. Confidence is a man-made trait that you must build within yourself. Encourage yourself, feel good about yourself and know that you have what it takes.

Do not ride the wave, create your own. The less people you deal with, the better. Keep certain people at a distance, and do not use the word *friend* loosely. People have ulterior motives, stay with the ones that stayed with you. Some people are like clouds, they disappear it is a beautiful day.

Procrastination

"You do not have to see the whole staircase. Just take the first step"
- Dr. Martin Luther King, Jr.

Procrastination is an enemy that we must defeat in order to prosper and be the best you. Excuses are never a good reason for not doing achieving. Why wait until tomorrow, when you can do it today? Tomorrow is not promised. You do not want to regret not achieving or experiencing something because of procrastination. The door of opportunity might close on you before you finally take the step to go through it. Take advantage of every opportunity. Time flies. You do not want to look back on your life years later down the line, wishing you accomplished everything you planned. It is either now or never. If you want something you have to go after it. Anything that comes too easy, is not worth having. Get

rid of the *I'll-do-it-later* mentality. Take charge of your life and your time, and do it now.

Do today what others will not so tomorrow you can reap the fruits of your labor of which others cannot. Stick with every plan you make and follow it through until completion. Practice makes perfect so if you practice at being a procrastinator you are going to be greatest procrastinator just like anything else you practice on. Do not watch it happen, make it happen for yourself. Big things have small and humble beginnings.

Assumptions

"Never make assumptions about someone based on your past experiences with someone else" - Unknown

Assumptions may be the beginning of an ending. It is easier to just ask a question if you are uncertain about something instead of trying to come up with the answer yourself without knowing the facts behind a situation. A lot of unnecessary stress and headache could be easily circumvented. When you do not know something, your mind starts racing a mile a minute and you come up with an elaborate imagination in your head. A vast majority of the time you are most likely wrong when you assume or speculate. Communication is the key so it is important to make sure you and everyone in the situation have a clear understanding and maintain

common ground. Nothing good comes from assuming someone of something they did not do. It makes everyone feel awkward. However, when you speak from fact, it puts everyone at ease including yourself.

To Observe Will not Hurt

"God gave us two ears and one mouth
for a reason." - John 1:19

No one knows it all. If you want to learn how to do something, watch. If you want to learn something, ask. There are times to speak and times to listen, it is imperative to know the difference. If you are talking then you are not actively listening, therefore missing out on an opportunity to learn something new and valuable. There is wisdom in listening.

People learn from their mistake, but wise people learn from the mistakes of others. You can learn something from every person you come across, whether it is something you want to avoid or something you want to want to pick up to emulate. Study and do your research on everything, whether it is a relationship or a job. People are creatures of habit; you can tell what

someone is about to do just by their previous patterns. Be cautious; never let your feelings think for you. Watch others so you will know what to do and what not to. Be willing to listen to others and be teachable. You are not right about everything, no one is. It takes courage to stand up and speak, it takes even more courage to open your mind and listen. Half of being smart is knowing what you are ignorant of.

Work Smart

"If you work hard and do your best,
you can do anything." - Unknown

Work smarter, not harder. A wise man once said that two jobs are for two people. The smart people try and decrease their labor hours so they can focus on their own personal goals and achievements. The long term goal should be to become an entrepreneur not only so you can have financial freedom but more importantly you can pass your businesses down to your children and grandchildren. The average millionaire has seven sources of income. Think outside the box. Do not let a $50,000 a year job stop you from making $50,000 a month. Patience is a virtue. Work smart, make every moment count. Do not do anything yourself when you can get someone to do it for you, two heads are better than one. Everyone has a role and position to

play. Make a living doing what you love. If you do, it will not seem nor feel like work.

Break Bad Habits

"Bad habits are easier to abandon today than tomorrow." - Proverb

Habits are something we do subconsciously without thinking because we are so accustomed to doing them. It is important to replace bad habits with good ones. We all have a bad habit we need to lose. Whether your habit is procrastinating or losing focus. Forming better habits takes time and effort. Everything takes time and a lot of work. Important habits are vital to our success and achieving greatness. Our good habits and good practices will determine how far we go in life. In everything you do, you should be thinking long-term. Break the bad habits now so the good habits will be easier to follow later in the life. You will never change your life until you change your daily practice. The secret of your greatness is found in your daily

routine. Until you are willing to change your approach, your routine, you cannot improve your results.

Sacrifice

"We often forget that growth requires sacrifice." - Alberto Villoldo

Sacrificing means to give up something you have for something you want. You cannot be successful or the best you without sacrificing. We would all like to get something for nothing but unfortunately that is not how life works. People do not fail to be great, they fail to make the sacrifices in order to be great. Sacrifice is necessary if you want to reach the full level of your potential. There is nothing *easy* about being great. Greatness requires hard work, sleepless nights and early mornings.

Stay home focused on your craft while on your peers are out partying, doing the things you want to be doing. Always keep in mind that those who are out partying while your home working on your goals do not want it as bad as you. The party-clubs will be there 40 years from now so it can wait.

If you do not plan to sacrifice then you do not plan to be great. Great achievement always requires great sacrifice.

Discipline

"Discipline is the bridge between goals
and accomplishment." - Unknown

Self-discipline is one of the mandatory
traits you need to implement in order to be
great. Without discipline it is impossible to
achieve what you are capable of. Every great
person is utterly disciplined. They know how
to stay focused despite what is going on
around them. They are too focused doing
what is important to worry about what
everyone else is doing. Be patient, the best
things happen unexpectedly. You must have
the ability to control your impulses, emotions
and behaviors. You have to be able to turn
down immediate pleasure for long-term
goals.

Educate Yourself

"Education is the passport to the
future, for tomorrow belongs to those
who prepare for it today."
– Malcolm X

If you want to hide something from
someone, put it in a book. The average
person rarely reads, but reading is the
number one hobby of a millionaire. They are
valuable lessons, wisdom and knowledge
hiding inside the pages of books. With the
way technology is set up today you can just
Google whatever you are inquisitive of. You
do not have to go to college to be educated.
It is all about what you teach yourself. If you
do not educate yourself than your mind will
be stagnated. You will act the same way when
you are 51 as you did when you were 15.
Every day you just be willing and trying to

learn as much as you possibly can. No matter how much you already know you will never know it all.

During slavery, it was illegal for slaves to read because the masters were afraid of the slaves learning and becoming more superior than the masters. For centuries people knew the power hidden in books.

Have Faith

"Let your faith be bigger than your fears." - Unknown

Have faith that you can do anything you put your mind to. If you do not believe in yourself, no one else will. You have to always believe in God. He will not put you through anything you cannot handle. God gives His strongest battles to His strongest soldiers. Life does not come with a rulebook or guidelines on how to overcome obstacles, you just need faith and confidence in yourself. Have faith in the fact that you are exactly where God wants you. Do not let anyone convince you that you are not where God wants you. Rome was not built in one day. No matter how things look right now, know that God is still in control of our life. Stay in peace, and believe that He will always be with you in adversity and other

directions. If God does not give you what you want, it is not what you need.

Chase Your Dreams

"The biggest adventure you can take is
to live the life of your dreams."
- Oprah Winfrey

You can sleep and dream, or you can
wake up and chase them. Nothing worth
having is going to come easy. If you want
something you have to work for it. The
harder you work, the closer you will be in
conquering your dreams. Never stop, go for
what you want whether it is a new car or a
new life. Anything is possible if you are
willing to put the work in for it. Everyone is
different and has a unique talent. Figure out
what makes you different from everyone else.
You were put here for a reason. Never give
up on something you really want. It is
difficult to wait but worst to regret.

Productive Hobbies

"No one is really happy without a
hobby." - William Oslen

Find something you love to do;
something you do not mind doing for free.
Hobbies are a good balance in life and gives
you a peace of mind. Hobbies are beneficial
and have a great value in your everyday life.
They add value to us, and help us become
more efficient and productive. Hobbies are
also good for your health and spirit. By
indulging in hobbies, it takes our mind away
from our hectic schedules. Hobbies speak
volumes about who we are as person. Find
something you are passionate about and you
wouldn't mind doing for free. When you
finding a hobby that you love you will find a
side of yourself that you did not know exist.
It is important to take time out for ourselves.
When you have an excruciating day, your

hobbies are something

you can look forward to.

Weigh Your Options

"Things have a way of working out. Be patient." - Unknown

Never be too quick to make a decision, see what else there is out there. You might make a decision too quick, and something comes better the next. But you cannot take the offer, because you already decided to commit something else. Try not to pick a side if you can, stay independent and keep your options open at all times. You never know what is waiting for you; good things come to those who wait. The best is yet to come, just prepare yourself for it. Always think long term when it comes to committing to something or someone, or else your just wasting your time and energy into something you know is not

going to last.

Know Your Worth

"Sometimes you must forget what you feel and remember what you deserve."
- Unknown

We have all felt victimized by a friend or someone who we cared about. Everyone has been treated wrong. We have the tendency to blame others for the way they treat us. We all have choices, you never have to settle for less. Believe that you deserve more. Realize that the most important relationship you have is one with yourself. Embrace self-love and self-respect. Focus on constantly growing and transforming into the greatest you. If someone runs away from you when you are at your worst then do not even think about taking them back when you are at your best. You

cannot go back in time to correct your Mistakes. Be careful of who you invest or waste your time on and be selective. Love yourself in order to be loved.

Show respect and you will be respected. Most importantly, love and respect yourself first. Know your value and do not accept being treated less than you deserve. You deserve to be treated the way you treat others, and vice versa. Life is too short to settle for less, because you are too impatient to wait for what is best. The people in your past are in your past for a reason. Do not dwell on it or take them back because you feel lonely. It better to be alone and happy, instead of being with someone and hurting.

Ruffus. J. Yates, IV

Embrace The Struggle

"A smooth sea never made a skillful sailor." - Unknown

Struggle is part of the process to success. A person should not look at the struggle as a lose but as a lesson. Going through hard times builds character. Tough times do not last but tough people do. There is a bright light at the end of every dark tunnel. God's plan is always the best. Sometimes the process is painful and hard. Do not forget that when He's silent, He's doing something for you. Things happen to everyone, every day. The difference is how people deal with it. Difficult roads often lead to beautiful destinations. Remember this, someone took the same situation you are complaining about and won. What we often think of as defeat is really to make us better. You are exactly where you are supposed to be in life at this very moment. Every experience

is a part of God's plan. I never met a strong person with an easy past. Life does not get easier, you just get stronger.

Speak Highly Of Yourself

"Do not speak badly of yourself. For the warrior within hears your words and is lessened by them."
- David Gemell

What you think of yourself is much more important than what people think of you. If you do not talk good about yourself, nobody else will. What you put out into the universe, will return to you. You have to exude confidence and remind yourself that you were put on the earth for a reason. You are God's gift, and you were put on this earth to lift others. How can you lift others if you are perpetually putting yourself down? Once you start to accept and love yourself, the smoke will clear, and you will breathe easy again. Be kind to yourself and life will be a much brighter place for you.

Travel

"The word is a book, and those who
do not travel read only one page."
- Unknown

The world is like a big book, and if you do not open it and explore you will forever be stuck in the same place. The world has so much to offer, you have to go out and get it. Travel is one of the most profound ways to break a routine. It is an utterly a different world out there. The food, the people, the language. The new experience is most needed. You have to get out and travel as much as possible. The average round trip plane ticket is approximately $300. Majority of us spend that in a week on food. Traveling makes you humble. Get out every chance you get and see the rest of the world. Visit as many places as you can, take pictures and capture the moments. Even if you cannot afford a

plane ticket, take a road trip and see historical sites. It is a breath of fresh air when you go to a new place for the first time, it allows you forget all about the problems you left back at home.

Set Goals

"People with goals succeed because they know where They are going."
- Earl Nightingale

Goals are what motivates us to move forward in life. When you have a goal you will do anything necessary to achieve it, and you will have more of a reason to get up a little earlier each morning, or go to sleep a little later at night. A goal is just a wish with a deadline. You have to stay focused on your goals and once you achieve them, make a new one so you're always moving forward.

Do not Expect Handouts

"Earn it. It makes you appreciate it more." - Unknown

If you wait for someone to give you an opportunity, you will wait forever. You have to create your own opportunity and be in control of your own destiny. You cannot walk with your head high and your hand out. When you work hard for something, and get it on your own you appreciate it more. You have to be patient. When someone gives you something, you are in debt to them. Work hard for what you want so nobody can say "You wouldn't have that if it was not for me."

Never Look Back

"The only time you should look back,
is to see how far you've come."
- Unknown

Sometimes people do not notice the things we do for them until we stop doing them. Everything is in your past is there for a reason and if you try to back-track and relive it you will get the same thing. To do the same thing and expect different results is insanity. Never take things as a loss but a lesson learned instead. When you go through something you become wiser, utilize what you learned from the past and apply it to your future so you do not make the same mistakes twice. When you start to figure out what you want in life, there will be obstacles. Do not let anyone or anything discourage you from continuing on. Believe in yourself and believe in your decisions. Stay positive and keep moving

forward.

Stay Positive

"Once you replace negative thoughts
with positive ones, you will start
having positive results." - Willie
Nelson

In a world full of negativity it is hard to
stay positive. If it were easy to stay positive,
everyone would do it. Be a person that
inspire others to be better. Positive attitudes
lead to positive results. A compliment can go
a long way. Do not lose hope; not everyone
will see your vision. You attract who you are.
Positive people always have negative
thoughts, they just do not let those thoughts
control them. You cannot live a positive life

with a negative mind. The less you respond to negative people, the more positive your life will become. A positive

mind finds opportunity in everything. Likewise, a negative mind finds flaws in everything. Try to go without saying anything negative for 24 consecutive hours and watch your life change.

Nothing will slow your progress like a negative mindset, stay positive.

Train your mind to see the good in every situation. Be aware of how important words are in life and the effect they have on others. Look for something positive in each day, even if you have to look a little harder.

Think Before You Make A Move

"Before you say something, stop and think how you'd feel if someone said it to you." - Unknown

Life is like a game of chess, you should think before you move, try and visualize the outcome. Do not just do things because your bored, think long term. Weigh the pros and the cons. Think about who would be affected by the decision you are going to make. Never let your emotions supersede your intelligence. Everything should be meticulously calculated. Do everything for a reason. Always think about the worst that can happen. If you can live with the answer, than go for it. If not, simply walk away. You are free to make whatever choices you want, but you are not free from the consequences of your decisions.

Do What Makes You Happy

"Life is better when you do what makes you happy regardless of what others think. It is your life, not theirs."
- Sonya Parker

You should not do things to make someone else happy; they have a life of their own, they can do what makes them happy. Focus on yourself and do what makes you happy. Being miserable and stressful cuts your life short. Whether it is a job or a relationship, if it costs you your sanity and peace of mind than you cannot afford it. Find your passion. Nobody holds you back more than yourself. Do what you love. You should not regret having to go to work when your alarm goes off in the morning because you dread going to a job you hate. You should not dread going in the house after work to a relationship you hate. When you're passionate about a job you love, you will not need an alarm clock, you're enthusiastic to work and will happily wake you up in the morning. You will also lose the need to impress, please, and compare ourselves to other people. You cannot compare your Chapter one to someone else's Chapter 22.

As long as you are trying to compete, you will never be fully satisfied with yourself. Happiness does not come from pleasing others, it comes from pleasing yourself. Never base your life decisions on advice from people who do not have to deal with the results. The person who tries to keep everyone happy often ends up feeling the loneliest.

About The Author

Ruffus J. Yates, IV is a native of New York's Capital Region. Born in Albany, he attended St. Joseph's St. John's Academy in Rensselaer prior to relocating with his family to the Greater Atlanta region where he attended Gwinnett County Public Schools. He later graduated from Job Corps in Brunswick, Georgia at 16.

With New York in his heart, Ruffus relocated back to Albany and at 17 enrolled in Hudson Valley Community College where he majored in Human Services. As life would have it, his plans were rerouted to an unplanned path.

After four years of re-focusing, Ruffus changed his mindset, his path and embarked on a new direction. He enrolled in college and graduated from Brandford Hall's medical assistant program.

Ruffus is now a Registered Medical Assistant and part-time basketball coach. During his leisure time, he enjoys watching sports, cooking, fishing, riding dirt bikes, and reading books.

Ruffus has proven that with focus, determination and vision, you can achieve *greatness.*

NOTES

NOTES

Ruffus. J. Yates, IV

Greatness Is A Process

Ruffus. J. Yates, IV

Greatness Is A Process

Made in the USA
Las Vegas, NV
11 April 2021